Unplanned Mystery

AFZA KULSUM

PAPER TOWNS
PUBLISHERS

First Published by
Paper Towns Publishers
72, Vishwanath Dham Colony,
Niwaru Road, Jhotwara,
Jaipur, 302012

Unplanned Mystery

ISBN Print Book - 978-93-6185-901-4

Printed in India

DEDICATION

To all those young selves,
To enticing kinships,
To endless beginnings,
To life's epitomes,
And
To all unplanned mysteries!

!

Unplanned Mystery

CONTENTS

Unplanned Mystery

EPIGRAPH

"From Us She wandered now a Year,
Her tarrying, unknown,
If Wilderness prevent her feet
Or that Ethereal Zone"

-Emily Dickinson

Unplanned Mystery

PREFACE

Coming home
And finding her napping
Peacefully
Forever
On the old wooden sofa
With a note in her hand that says
I love you child
In that shaky handwriting
Written with a broken pencil

Coming home
And finding her napping:
My favorite food ready on the table
Coffee to reduce my stress
And when I tiptoe to not wake her
up

She blurts out and asks
"Did you finish the food"?

Coming home
And finding her colourful sarees
drying
In every corner of the house.
I pat my head and chuckle at her
innocence
"There is a drying stand"
I say and she unmistakably
apologizes zillions of times.
Like every evening, she says
"Oh dear! I'm sorry I forgot"

Coming home
And finding her solace
In her happy little world
Just another day-
Her laughter still echoes
Her words still soothe

Her memories keeping her world
jubilant
I realize she is in a better place
And cheer up when she's smiling at
me from heaven Memories prick
but memories bring time alive.
I miss you Nani!

INTRODUCTION

Do you sometimes feel like
everything is planned, but nothing
works?
You may sometimes wonder what
life has in store for you-something
out of the box, but mostly
unplanned.

Every tale has a twist,
and I'm gonna take you-
on a jaw-dropping journey;

A twisted tale,
A car with no brakes,
A never ending roller coaster ride,
A smile on every face.
Here's to Unplanned Mystery!

Unplanned Mystery

PROLOGUE

"Time favored me into my chime
Something that I love to do
Somewhere that I admire the view
Surfing the battle against my rattle.
Among the essence of beauty,
Fighting my sheer insanity.
The strength of my core,
The enigma of my roar,
My fancy to explore
And my aim to reach the shore!"

- (The Paradigm of my Destiny)

Unplanned Mystery

FOREWORD

The steps that we take often make us feel we've been going around in circles.
But that is the biggest tragedy of life, isn't it?
What is fruitful is always boring. The key is to be bored. The keys is to be persistent. The key is to show up every single day without failing and putting in the work.

And once you do that, the power of compounding emerges. All your efforts, all those sleepless nights- finally show you why you started.

One poem at a time. One paragraph at a time. Writing, tossing it in the bin- writing again. Getting disheartened, but trying again and trying harder.

And it's truly fulfilling recalling all those memories and writing this foreword to the book you always dreamed of. You did go around in circles, but just

look back at it- you came a long way!

And I am confident that "Unplanned Mystery" although amazing, is just a beginning. You have so much more to tell, to write, and to sing and we all want to, we all have to vibe to your tunes.

Here's to all those books!

And this toast I hope inspires you to work harder and give us the next book real soon, I am looking forward to it already!

It's your story- finally with the rest of us!

-Anuj Dubey
September 17th, 2023

Checkmate

I thought the world wasn't
trustworthy.
Fear, rogue, rejections, agony, loss
And all the negativity out there
Wasn't enough to bring out my dry
tears.
Yes, dry.
Dry because I was tired.
Dry because I was
Exhausted from accepting the
truth.

Life took unrealistic turns when
I had just started to realize
Or rather fathom the definition of
"simple"
Life was simple.
I was simple.
He was simple.
We together were simple.

Hah, but I guess a game of chess
was better to understand
where you're the master of your
own game.

The Flower of my life bloomed
When I was in grade 10,
From the little exchange of glances
Caught in the classroom,
Sharing food from each other's
lunch boxes,
Taking each other's note
When one is absent to class
To making plans of

How to copy in the examinations,
Everything was perfect.
Perfection had to never cease
But little did I know
That I had to live in dreams.

Dreams come true.
My dream of leaning on his
shoulders
And feeling protected had come
true.
My dream of feeling the warmth
On his shoulders had come true.
Maybe we both had the same
dreams.
But our dreams chose different
paths.

Checkmate!
He was a master of his game of
chess.
The terrorists were his pawns

And he was the king of defense.
He leaned on his own shoulders.
The country leaned on his
 shoulders.
I had been sleeping on his
 shoulders in my dreams
When I realized that world wasn't
 trustworthy.

ΔΔΔ

Gusto of love

My eyes gave me jitters
And my heart skipped a beat
When I first saw him
Butterflies were churning my
 stomach
Until the sand of my agitation
Sunk out of the hourglass.
The clock struck 12 of my most
 earnest day.
The flashback of his cutest smiles
Led my eyes blinking
And the melody of his hoarse
Yet sweetest voice
Continued ringing bells in my ears.

Seventh heaven described my heart
When it was time for me to turn
My beloved to my inamorato
I knew for a fact that
I couldn't afford to lose him
 because
I loved him with all my heart.

He helped me
He helped me turn my exhaustion
Into zest
He helped me turn
My spirits of hatred
Into droplets of love.
Oh!
He is my heart-throb.

The day he was mine,
I evoked into cloud nine.
My excitement was seen

By acquaintances,
By intruders,
By wanderers,
By elopers.
Thanatophobia engulfed me
When I was away from him
Yet I promised
I would love him
With all my heart
And the gusto of love would never
 clip to bits!

ΔΔΔ

Cupcake

I sit beside him and smile till my
cheeks turn pink
I sit beside him and wonder how he
makes my heart sink
He puts me in a dilemma or rather
castles in air
And I happen to twist my fingers in
my hair.

The feeling is weirdly beautiful.
It seems like butterflies are having
sex in my tummy
Do I like that feeling?
Or do I cry
"Oh Mummy!"

His arms calm my anxious zest
But my mind turns the moment
Into an obnoxious fest
Yet, his arms are all I need
His cute names melt me indeed

A tired day and frustration out of sight
But his voice seems to set everything right
"My mini cupcake" he says
And I ideally shy away.

ΔΔΔ

Frozen space

Tranquility down the lane,
I find my mind in a frozen space.
I savor my few hours of solitude,
In the beauty of nature and it's
grace.

The soft breeze hits my face
And my smile curves up like a
bracket.
I settle to pen down my reflection,
When the sky clusters my mind's
casket.

I am desperate to explore the
quintessence of
Mother Nature,
She never fails to intrigue me
With her charm,
As I happen to falter.

I admire his creation,
It puts me to solace
And this comfort, nobody can
 replace,
As I go back to my frozen space.

I find my surroundings still, at no
 pace
I grin at my clever mother,
Mother Nature,
Who drove me through radiant
 thoughts,
Like a feather.

ΔΔΔ

Amigo

You blink at my imagination,
Sit still for my hooey conversation.
The Jerry in my life to quarrel and
spat
And someone to have the most
fascinating chat.

Laughter till my stomach held
burning coals,
And tickle me until my body rolls.
Endless gossips and browsing
recipes
Only to finally cook maggi, the
classic recipe.

Disliking the same person
And smirking faces,
When one gets a new best friend
Oh, Roasting is the Gen-Z way to
befriend.

Twinning outfits,
Clicking pictures, posting on
Instagram
Hey, suggest me a caption for the
gram!

Hah! 10 years down the line,
I'll hug you like a burrito
And everytime I see you,
I'll never forget to say
"Hola Amigo!"

ΔΔΔ

Oh Darlin'!

Sky is your limit ?
Trying to burst the myth?

Oh Darlin'!
Dreams have no limit.
Fly with your wings,
Dream to achieve,
It's okay to fail,
Because you are an elastic.

Oh Darlin'!
Title yourself.
You are the interesting story
And the world is your reader
The prologue maybe harsh,
Happy that the Americans want,

A French-like life,
Or as boring as ketchup on Maggi.
But the title captures attention.

Oh Darlin'!
Twist your tale.
Night is no beautiful without stars
And you are just boring
without an exciting twist.

Climb the Himalayas of your
journey,
Or rappel down the zip-line.
It's your adventure.
Let that leech creep you,
Let that rock scrape you,
Cry a little, laugh a little,
Oh Darlin'!
You are the writer of your story.

ΔΔΔ

The wine of life

Sometimes you feel animosity
When sometimes it's just pure curiosity
Sometimes you may have to let go
but the pain is worth an avalanche
You may cry, you may catch it like a little baby's grip
Or you may bare it with life's little sips.

Well, life is tiny gravels by the riverside
Beautiful, yet ailing when you walk on the bare sides.
It's like a hanging ladder at an altitude
Breathtaking, yet you fall at your bad mood.

You may have to fly
To coop the experience on the other side,
Go through the rile,
Ring the blues among the hues,
Emerge in fine feather despite the terrible weather,
And life will succeed after the heed.

ΔΔΔ

The Paradigm of my destiny

I realized the paradigm of my destiny when the sky turned deep orange.
The sunset,
The waves,
The breeze and my curly hair were all I knew.
The waves swaying in my mind,
And the waves of the sea seemed to relate
Just like the colors violet, indigo, blue, green, yellow, orange and red.
Oh! Did I just mention the rainbow?
Cause I can now see a beautiful spectrum amidst the tangelo.

My eyes were awestruck and my
jaws wide open when I realized the
paradigm of my destiny.

The earth so beautiful and my
freedom yelling echoed ecstasy
My heart so warm although the
space is a freezing melody.
My arms flying like a bird's remedy
And my mind calm like a
psychological therapy
Will I ever want to go back to
where I came from?
Not now, not ever.

I realized the paradigm of my
destiny when my apocalypse ruined
the good time
But time favored me into my chime
Something that I love to do
Somewhere that I admire the view
Surfing the battle against my rattle.

Among the essence of beauty,
fighting my sheer insanity.
The strength of my core,
the enigma of my roar,
my fancy to explore
and my aim to reach the shore
They do not die!

They do not die, cause my core
holds all the pressure on that
surfboard.
The pressure of life, the pressure of
my carte blanche and the pressure
of people uncovered.
I realized the paradigm of my
destiny
When the realm of existence would
envy me
but the 'Past Young ME' would be
proud of me.
I see you with my spiral eye
Just like you see me through the
painting and sigh!

The Devil and the Moon

Maybe the world wants you.

You are broken battling a
war against yourself
trying to put those little broken
pieces together.
The Devil of your conscience is
trying to lay you off guard
While the angelic moon wants
to keep you focused

The suspense in your heart is
twinkling
like a glint from the magic wand
while you are struck with that
ominous anxiety.

You let out a sigh of whimper,
to slow sobs and blubber like a
baby
when the devil returns with a
wicked
"You are broken, nothing can fix
you".
'Oh Honey! This anguish is only
temporary.
Stop listening to the cruel dark devil
and stay focused'
the sweet moon quibbles.

'You' are important
amid these mixed brawls and the
final essence
'cause, the World wants You!

Strange connection

It was mid-evening,
when she was singing down the
street.

Her tune jingled around,
and softly swayed into the ears of
the locals.

She tickled pink,
and began her unprecedented
journey.

The journey of friendship,
that was strangely made.

She laid bewildered engrossed in enigma,
but the darkness around pegged her.

She found peace across the night,
and that beauty enthralled her sight.

She strange connection is now part of her life,
The night will never leave her like the friend and the strife.

ΔΔΔ

Mistakes leave Scars

I tried.
Every minute I tried.
But apologizes are not treasured
I thought it's all back to normal.
I thought we were friends again.
Little did I know that my words
would create blunder
I struggle, rough and tumble
Until I cry.

My heart aches when I realize
that the same bond will never come
back.
I tried to correct my mistake.
I tried to put it all together

Our friendship, our bond, our trust
But it flew with the dust.
Well, my heart still aches because I tried.
Every minute I tried.

I know she tried.
But I was blind
I know she apologized
But I didn't think beyond my mind.
I believed someone I shouldn't have.
I quarreled with someone I shouldn't have.
I cried too.
I tried too .

Maybe it was never meant to be.
Maybe I expected a lot towards
me.
From her, from her friendship, until
I set her free.
I nudged a third eye and when she
went away I sighed
Not with relief, but a doze of pain
and cry.

Fancy Time

From austere thoughts to
random imagination,
Wanting to face every typical
situation,
3 Am is that fancy time,
Where sober thoughts flood my
mind.

The endless conversation of the
day,
The sight of the serene night,
Attack my dopy eyes,
And my heart reluctantly cries.

I regret my past,
But I remember that those are days that have passed.
So I think about this overwhelming appreciation for the love of my life,
But my mind brings me to the bitter strife.

My friend "career" knocks the door of my brain,
But appearing at 3 AM makes him so inhumane.

I wish I had the superpower to travel the world for free,
So that I can go on my favorite shopping spree.

I then try to sleep,
Despite the thoughts that have gone deep.
But 3am is so intimidating ,
That makes my night all the more interesting.

ΔΔΔ

Frenzied Fantasy

Fantasy and irony coming across
I wish I could be in a different
world,
A world filled with desires and
frenzy
But my fantasy is not able to get
through the waves, The waves of
snag,
The waves of life.

A mermaid in my mind and
obnoxious dreams

How I wish I lead a life as
unwinding as a mermaid- Fantasy,
reverie and the blue sea.
But the waves are my stumbling
block
Not allowing me to live like
the mermaid.

I try hard to push the waves,
So hard that they reach the sky
Where my limit has no bound
And I make my mark
Just like those stars in the limitless
sky.

Yet, reality jolts me
And I'm coerced to come back
from my fantasy
To a world away from the
mermaid.
I am coerced to wake up the
dreaming mermaid in my dream

To stop her from setting my bars.
I don't want my dream to be
hampered by the obnoxious little
mermaid in my hallucination
Because the little fishes might only
nudge me with their tiny fins
But my aim is much more than the
only sea.

A world away from the sea is my
world
And the dream unlike the
mermaid's dream is my dream.
A dream of reality and a dream
unlike desires.

ΔΔΔ

The Nightmare

She kept aside her sleeping pills
Hoping for a peaceful night
She took a deep breath,
heaved a sigh of relief ,
sent a silent prayer to god,
and slept cozily like the slow
sinking sun at dusk ,
when suddenly an eccentric fear
agitated her.
Anxiety struck her like the arrow on
the target.
It was the scariest night she ever
felt.

She could sense her father's soul
and was in a dilemma if spirits exist.
Petrifying thoughts wandered
around her inner space.
She was disturbed and her wish to
sleep well was gradually waning

"I hate night time" she screamed.
'Ahhhhh'
she was filled with horror.
She wanted to give up,
She wanted to lose herself.
A night without pills reminisces her
worst nightmare.

She recalled her father's death,
she recalled every second of that
night.
Oh darling! It is a delusion.
Fathers don't harm.
They want you to be the best
the best at every step.

Womanhood

I am an endless ocean,
Deep but calm.

With my unselfish love,
I welcome you to my shore.

I am like that taxi,
Who can take you along,
And wait until eternity,
Without any fare or charges.

I am called an emotional wreck,
Where if I am protective, I'm called
insecure,
And if I am insecure,
I am called possessive.

Do I not have the right to love?
Do I not have the right to live?

I am neither time nor river,
To not wait for my family.

I am happy to take up my responsibilities,
I am happy with the beautiful 9-month phase,
Well, I am a desert where you will find an oasis on searching patiently.

My love is unconditional,
Only if you open your clumsy mind,
I am made to love, live and run the world,
With not only my duties but also dignity.

I am a WOMAN.
And I am a human too!

The Monsters

She strolled around the street
Believing that she was safe

She was dressed in a Salwar
Believing she was dressed decently.

Hundreds of dreams in mind
One goal to achieve

She set past her fear
To achieve what she believed

But Alas!

The worst had to happen
The monsters had to attack

Unable to give in to their lust
They rolled their tongues out

To brutalize her
To scar her

Her dreams were dead
Her beliefs were dead

Her entire journey flipped!

The monsters are still alive!
The bitter truth and sad reality

The world wants to speak up,
The world wants to change

Well, the monsters are still alive!

ΔΔΔ

Breathe

Breathe in, Breathe out
Breathe in, Breath out.
Sigh! It didn't help her.
Trauma? Panic? Hassle?
She couldn't figure it out.

Her mind was in a frenzy of emotions,
Sometimes happy like the bright smiling sun
Or sometimes depressing like a gloomy weather.
She was yearning for a tight hug or perhaps hands to hold
But most of the times, she chose to be reclusive.

What has the monster done?
Abandoned her happy senses?
Nastily trying to desert her peace of mind?
Xany spirit died away?

Intuitions always driving towards negativity?
Emotions going crazy?
Tears everyday?
Yearning for distraction and some happiness forever?

Oh! Anxiety is a monster.
She lost herself in the process of getting rid of her anxiety.
But not anymore.
She did whatever she loved to do
But said NO to Anxiety.

The Daily Evil

It was pitch dark
When I tried to find a little spot of light
But a thud caught my ears
Giving way from my only source
Maybe it is my delusion,
An aroma in the senses of my brain
The evil succeeded in trapping me
Leading my coward heart
To a galore of imaginations
It felt like a catastrophe by the evil
Trying to hold me back from my victory
My fear was instinct with horror
But the evil didn't seem to care
It was winning and so was my delusion
I loathe the evil,
The Evil called "Distraction".

Grotesque

Beyond the school,
Across the river,
Beyond my house,
I broke the 'rule'.

Thatched roof,
Three hens,
He broke an egg,
Omelette, a tasteless proof.

A walk to the woods,
Creepy insects,
Ghost myths,
Just like horror books.

A wide space,
Dark sky,
Soothing breeze,
Yet, a scary place.

A little strolling
And a broken bridge,
Jump high across,
The land left us unrolling.

What now?
Where are we headed?
What's life?
Or is the view just wow?

The mountain on the other side,
The river gushing through,
Eagles swirling around,
But there's nowhere to hide.

A wooden boat,
Old and timid,
Unsure yet rowed the oar,
Our eyes beamed when we saw the coast.

A little 24 hour trek,
Life and death in our hands,
Finally we find the monk,
A little holy, a little more fake.

The monk smiled,
Fed us food,
Hugged us warm
"Are you happy my child?"

We nodded
Admiring the cave,
Gold and diamonds,
Sparking among the darkest.

The monk speaks
Why are you here?
What about your school and home?
His tongue he sheepishly clicks.

School is bad, I say
I have no home, he says.
The monk's eyes twinkle,
"Come with me" the monk says.

A golden door,
Paintings and crafts,
"Damn" a word slips,
Surprised at what was in store.

Another door,
Candies and juice,
Books and colors,
Something to adore.

A third door,
The selfish brass tacks,
Our eyes wide open,
Never seen it before.

Monk, the son of god?
The crying, hungry children

What were they doing there?
Monk, the monster of the squad?

Eclipsed Despair

To the dawn or back to the
midnight?
Insomnia or just the everyday
fright?

She could sense the shiver down
her spine
When she saw him, hanging just
fine.

The note in red opened her beaded
eyes
The cold room gave way to a
thousand mice.

She pulled his legs but in vein,
The strings pulled him up with
now, the painless chain

Why did he do it?
No one knows or rather he just
froze

Knock knock, who's there?
Not anymore. Can my ears bare?

The sharpest ears couldn't hear the
sharpest shrill
Suicide or murder?
His death still gives her chills

ΔΔΔ

Infinite Amore

The old ties of love
To a fresh bond till doomsday.
The best antiques from left field
journeys,
And hands to hold for the
cherishing warmth.
Angels in disguise they are, saviors
in our life they are.
Ten letters worth a King's ransom
Incomparable to anything less
precious.
You cede your trust into them,
You share the so-called cliched
“mutual understanding”,
Oh, how treasured! How priceless!
The ten lettered friendship-
An enticing kinship.

ΔΔΔ

The Boston Dream

Boston, I thought my life would be
complete.
Like every other teenager, I had my
bucket list.

Chilling in the fenway park,
Hotfoot the Boston marathon,
Going crazy with all my friends- uh
it's teenage afterall
And munching on the best snack
every sixtieth of hour.

Well, this is how I thought things for
me should go.
But the ideal adolescence always
blazes, isn't it?
Because my friends think that I am
the problem
I feel I'm dying while I am still alive
"Hey you, forgetful nerd" my friends
call me.

Forgetting forgetting forgetting,
"Ahhh!"
Is there any way I can remove that
word from the dictionary?
I feel like a far cry from my friends
I feel like a flying slipper approaching
me when they laugh at me.

I feel my name will soon be changed
from Ms Alexa to Ms forgetting,
Well, what I can do
If Alzeihmers in my mind and body
is celebrating a wedding!

Unsilenced Resignation

I quit". He said.
"HAHAHA"
"Hey Coward"
"You're a loser"

A flock of mockingbirds flew
towards him
A tale of objections rang bells into
his ears.
What could he do?
Beg mercy from the merciless?
Or cry the dried tears?

"Just another month"
"Oh poor boy"
"You cannot abscond"
"You foolish brat"

He was frazzled in just a month
"I don't like it", he said.
Quitting is for the coward.
Well, says who?
Cause' Quitting is brave.

"Explored enough?"
"Or still exploring?"
"I won't pay you"
"You are giving up"

Who are you?
His life? Or his mind?
A month or a year,
Quitting is okay,
Until…..

Echoes of sobs,
His body wrapped in a shroud
Mockingbirds grieving
Nobody knew,
Until…. He quit forever.

The Colorblind

The Colorblind,
Her masterpiece.

It was worth zillions ,
Her faith more than a trillion,
"I won't give up" she said,
"I will never give up" she believed.

Her fingers were beautifully curved
Her brushes had colors of the
universe
Her husband unraveling every
nervous nerve
Her coffee, her companion, next to
her canvas served.

Shades of emotion,
Unfolded like an ocean.

She had a colorful hue
On her black board, darkness in view
"Why is she wasting time?" mockeries at queue,
"Well, you will see", her rage flew.

And finally it's that day
And there's no more dismay
And the jealous crowd turns grey
When the canvas is on display

MonaLisa by Da Vinci,
The Colorblind from Kentucky.

Her eyes were absent from sight,
Her brain did all the might
Her brushes always stroke right
The Colorblind because she was
blind.

ΔΔΔ

Where do I belong?

I wish to lead but I'm afraid,
of my plight and quandary.

I live in my mind's prodigy,
Filling every checkbox that I'm asked,
But blanched into reality in my gritty style.

"Speak your heart" my conscience says to me,
When I am drenched in day-daydreaming,
About my mistakes and snafu,
And cry over spilled milk.

Where do I belong?

In the highway of life?

Or in the reality rearmed in my senses.
Checkbox check, flair check!
The life that I live in photos?
Or the life without filters.

Where do I belong?

Oh! I belong in myself.
My young, spry, nervous self.
A stew of poetry in mind,
A prose-like heart,
A metaphoric body.
I belong in my vivacious poetic self!

Epilogue

"Life, he realized was much like a song. In the beginning, there is mystery, in the end there is confirmation, but it's the middle where all the emotion resides to make the whole thing worthwhile."

-Nicholas Sparks

Afterword

"Dear young me,
You hold a significant place,
At every single phase of life.
You are like a bed of bed of flowers,
Pretty and beautiful,
That can make your life meaningful.
People may come and go,
But the ones who stay,
Will never make you feel low.
Don't take life too seriously
Because it's a basket of mysteries.
Find fun in whatever you do,
Bunk few classes and enjoy the view.
Stand tall and different,
I'd love to see you grow,
Don't get carried away young one,
Enjoy and have absolute fun!"

-Afza Kulsum

Learning to finesse through her ups and downs, a young mind shaping into a matured soul, a girl turning into a woman through words, and her world- her poetry. She is Afza. She is a budding poet and she weaves poetry through the things she sees inspiration in. She believes that poetry is about feelings.